GEORGE GERSHWIN AT THE PIANO

10 SONG HITS

THE CHAPPELL AUTHENTIC

George Gershwin

EDITION

© 2006 by Faber Music Ltd
First published by International Music Publications Ltd
International Music Publications Ltd is a Faber Music company
Bloomsbury House 74–77 Great Russell Street London WC1B 3DA
Printed in England by Caligraving Ltd
All rights reserved

ISBN10: 0-571-52575-X
EAN13: 978-0-571-52575-1

To buy Faber Music publications or to find out about the full range of titles available,
please contact your local music retailer or Faber Music sales enquiries:

Faber Music Ltd, Burnt Mill, Elizabeth Way, Harlow, CM20 2HX England
Tel: +44(0)1279 82 89 82   Fax: +44(0)1279 82 89 83
sales@fabermusic.com   fabermusic.com

2

Love Walked In
(from the picture "Goldwyn Follies")

Music and Lyrics by GEORGE GERSHWIN and
IRA GERSHWIN

I Was Doing All Right

(from the picture "Goldwyn Follies")

Music and Lyrics by GEORGE GERSHWIN and
IRA GERSHWIN

45174

Love Is Here To Stay

(from the picture "Goldwyn Follies")

Music and Lyrics by GEORGE GERSHWIN and
IRA GERSHWIN

Nice Work If You Can Get It

(from the picture " Damsel In Distress')

Music and Lyrics by GEORGE GERSHWIN and
IRA GERSHWIN

Summertime
(Lullaby)
(from "Porgy And Bess")

By
GEORGE GERSHWIN, DUBOSE and
DOROTHY HEYWARD and IRA GERSHWIN

45174

12

45174

I Got Plenty O' Nuttin'

(from "Porgy And Bess")

By
GEORGE GERSHWIN, DUBOSE and
DOROTHY HEYWARD and IRA GERSHWIN

They Can't Take That Away From Me

From the picture "Shall We Dance"

Music and Lyrics by GEORGE GERSHWIN and
IRA GERSHWIN

Let's Call The Whole Thing Off

(From the picture "Shall We Dance")

Music and Lyrics by GEORGE GERSHWIN and
IRA GERSHWIN

They All Laughed

From the picture "Shall We Dance"

Music and Lyrics by GEORGE GERSHWIN and
IRA GERSHWIN

A Foggy Day

(from the picture "Damsel In Distress")

Music and Lyrics by GEORGE GERSHWIN and
IRA GERSHWIN